First World War
and Army of Occupation
War Diary
France, Belgium and Germany

1 CAVALRY DIVISION
Headquarters, Branches and Services
Royal Army Medical Corps
Assistant Director Medical Services
15 August 1914 - 12 October 1914

WO95/1101/2

The Naval & Military Press Ltd
www.nmarchive.com
Published in association with The National Archives

Published by

The Naval & Military Press Ltd

Unit 10 Ridgewood Industrial Park,

Uckfield, East Sussex,

TN22 5QE England

Tel: +44 (0) 1825 749494

www.naval-military-press.com

www.nmarchive.com

This diary has been reprinted in facsimile from the original. Any imperfections are inevitably reproduced and the quality may fall short of modern type and cartographic standards.

© **Crown Copyright**
Images reproduced by permission of The National Archives, London, England, 2015.

Contents

Document type	Place/Title	Date From	Date To
Heading	WO95/1101/2		
Heading	BEF 1 Cavalry Division C.R.A. 1914 Aug-1914 Oct		
Heading	1st Cavalry Divisional Artillery. Disembarked Havre 16.8.14 C.R.A. 1st Cavalry Division. August & September 1914		
War Diary		15/08/1914	03/09/1914
War Diary		02/09/1914	30/09/1914
Heading	1st Cavalry Divisional Artillery. C.R.A. 1st Cavalry Division. 1st to 12th October 1914		
War Diary		01/10/1914	12/10/1914

DO 95/1101/2

BEF

1 CAVALRY DIVISION

CRA RHA

1914 AUG – 1914 OCT

1st Cavalry Divisional Artillery.

Disembarked Havre 16.8.14.

C. R. A.

1st CAVALRY DIVISION.

AUGUST & SEPTEMBER 1914.

WAR DIARY
or
INTELLIGENCE SUMMARY.
(Erase heading not required.)

Army Form C. 2118.

1 Cav. Div. Arty.

Instructions regarding War Diaries and Intelligence Summaries are contained in F. S. Regs., Part II. and the Staff Manual respectively. Title pages will be prepared in manuscript.

Hour, Date, Place	Summary of Events and Information	Remarks and references to Appendices
Saturday August 15th 3.45 a.m.	Entrained at FARNBOROUGH Stn for SOUTHAMPTON. Embarked on Minneapolis for HAVRE. Arrived off HAVRE about 9 p.m. Stay outside till morning	
Sunday August 16 5 a.m.	Disembarked at HAVRE disembarkation completed at noon - D & E Batteries RHA arrived late in Evening	
Monday August 17	In billets at HAVRE	
12 midnight	Entrained at HAVRE	
Tuesday Aug 18th	Arrived at MAUBERGE 6 p.m. and proceeded to billets Hq Staff only	
Wednesday Aug 19th	In billets MAUBERGE.	
Thursday Aug 20th	Marched Hq Staff to AIBES where Cav Div Artillery Concentrated 5th Cav Bde. including J. Battery & Amm Column attached to Divn.	
Friday Aug 21st	Marched to GIVRY & the Artillery was then to continue march to HARMINIES where 7th & 3rd Bdes bivouacked	
Saturday Aug 22nd	5th Cav Bde no longer under orders of G.O.C. Cav Divn. The Division relieved by Infantry Outposts of the 2nd Army on the line GIVRY - MONS canal bridge at NIMY westward N of THULIN. The enemy became active in neighbourhood	

WAR DIARY
or
INTELLIGENCE SUMMARY.

(Erase heading not required.)

Army Form C. 2118.

Hour, Date, Place	Summary of Events and Information	Remarks and references to Appendices
Saturday Aug 22nd	of BLANCHE about noon + were ~~supported~~ engaged by the 5th Bde supported by D+E Batteries in action E of BRAY with the 7th Bde in readiness. No Casualties to men E Battery had a horse hit. The Cav Div: Arty then went into billets at QUIEVRAIN	
Sunday Aug 23rd	In billets till 5pm when I Battery RHA was detached & sent to IVth Cav Bde at ESTREUX. At 9 p.m the 7th & 3rd Bde [less I Battery] moved to a position on the high ground N of ANGRE from whence they advanced to WIHERIES arriving at 5.a.m 24th 7th & 13th Bde Am Col: moved to a posn S of BAISEUX with orders to retire on JENLAN.	
Monday Aug 24th	HQrs moved to ELOUGES at 1 am. The Cav Divn were engaged by Germans on the line CRESPIN + THULIN. L Battery came in action & shelled enemy successfully 1 mile N of AUDREGNIES + then retired with 2nd Cav Bde on AUDREGNIES about 8.a.m The Cav Divn was retiring in direction ROMBIES when G.O.C. got an urgent message from G.O.C. 5th Divn stating he was heavily engaged on his left flank. Whole Division returned and attacked enemy N to form line AUDREGNIES – ANGRE. 2nd Cav Bde supported by L Battery at woods just S.E AUDREGNIES charged in direction of ELOUGES + WIHERIES suffered heavily "L" Battery had 1 officer wounded & 5 other ranks with many (number uncertain) missing. D + E Battery came into different position	

WAR DIARY or INTELLIGENCE SUMMARY.

Army Form C. 2118.

(Erase heading not required.)

Hour, Date, Place	Summary of Events and Information	Remarks and references to Appendices
Monday Aug 24th (continued)	on line ANGRE + OMNEZIES + suffered no loss but did some visibly strong Execution. There was a difficulty in getting L Battery away, they were exposed to a very severe shell fire. The retirement was carried out in orderly manner successfully. The Divn retired for the night to neighbourhood of WARGNIES Le GRAND — and Le PETITE with HQ at PREUX au SART.	
Tuesday Aug 25th	Cav. Divn was divided into 2 Columns. Westerly Col 3rd + 4th BdEs under Gen Allenby. 1st + 2nd BdEs Easterly Column under Gen Briggs. with Cav. Divnl Arty Gen I Battery RHA. The lots were ordered to retire Westerly Col via ARMERIES + BERMERAIN. Easterly Col via RUESNES to VERTAIN. Arty HQs with E column. were ordered to make Le CATEAU at 5 pm in neighbourhood of SOLESMES. The rearguard were slightly engaged during day & the W. Column were heavily engaged near JENLAIN about 8 a m & near SOLESMES about 6 p m. E Column marched all night - through Le CATEAU + bivouacked for 2 hours near HONNECHY.	
Wednesday Aug 26th	Received supplies at 5 am + Gen Briggs recd an urgent message from Gen Ferguson asking for support on his right flank near Le CATEAU. which was promised. The action fought this day is entirely separately	App. A.

WAR DIARY
or
INTELLIGENCE SUMMARY.
(Erase heading not required.)

Army Form C. 2118.

APPENDIX A

Summary of the action of 1st Cav Div Arty at the action fought on line LIGNY & LE CATEAU on August 26th.

With Col. Briggs Column there was E battery & L Battery R.H.A. & about 12 noon Gen Gough with 3rd Bde and D battery less 1 Section, joined Gen Briggs. L Battery & 1 Sect D battery were with Gen Allenby 1st & 2nd Bde at Ligny.

Gen Briggs took up a defensive position N. of ESCAUFOURT & E of HONNICHY, pushing forward very wide patrols to the N and E. L Battery was brought into action in this position with E battery in action covering the long valley up to HONNICHY station. About 11.15 a.m. L Battery started shelling Enemy's guns near village of St SOMPLET and eventually pushed Mr Campbell's Section right forward to guard & watch the approaches from the village. At about 2 p.m. the guns were heavily engaging the infantry columns & guns advancing Westwards towards the right of the position. Gen Briggs pushed E battery up to support L and for 2 hours the batteries successfully checked this advance. The enemy continued to push on in spite of heavy casualties and about 4 p.m. owing to an aeroplane reconnaissance the guns were subjected to a very heavy shell fire – Explosive shells being used almost entirely. G.O.C. decided to retire Mr Campbell's section of L which was got back under very heavy shell fire with a few casualties. The remainder of L battery & E battery covered this withdrawal & then retired through village of ESCAUFOURT on to the high ground E of road from HONNICHY to BUSIGNY. Covered by the fire of the 2nd & 3rd Cav Bdes. which retired up the valley to HONNICHY Stn. The guns did not fire again. One wagon was hit and broken in the village and a few horses or men wounded slightly. The force then withdrew via BUSIGNY – BOHAIN – BRANCOURT – MONTBRAIN to RAMICOURT where it bivouacked for the night. E Battery joined 3rd Bde with 1 sect of D. 3rd Bde contains D & E Batteries, less 1 Sect, with 1st Bde.

WAR DIARY or INTELLIGENCE SUMMARY.

Army Form C. 2118.

(Erase heading not required.)

Hour, Date, Place	Summary of Events and Information	Remarks and references to Appendices
Thursday Aug 27th	Left RAMICOURT at 4 a.m. and retired towards St QUENTIN - covering the retirement of the 3rd & 5th Divisions. Covered the approaches to the town from the high ground S of St QUENTIN and billets in SERAUCOURT.	
Friday Aug 28th	Advanced to high ground S.W. St QUENTIN at 4 a.m. & picked up the many stragglers of the 3rd & 5th Divs & in the evening retired by St SIMON - CUGNY - to BERLANCOURT and St PLESSIS where the Bdes billeted. Gen De Lisle took over Command of the 2nd Bde.	
Saturday Aug 29th	At 9 a.m. 2nd Bde became heavily engaged by dismounted cavalry and guns. Gen Bupp moved up to support on the high ground W of BERLANCOURT. Both Brigades then fought a delaying action back to the ridge due S of line GUISCARD - BUCHOIRE where the Bdes took up a strong position astride main road S to NOYON. 2nd Bde W 1st Bde E of road with L Battery in action under cover E of the road. The force here with very accurate shell fire held the enemy till about 4.30 pm when the force retired on NOYON covered by the 14th Inf Bde. The enemy got their guns on the position vacated & shelled the	

WAR DIARY
or
INTELLIGENCE SUMMARY.

(Erase heading not required.)

Army Form C. 2118.

Hour, Date, Place	Summary of Events and Information	Remarks and references to Appendices
Saturday Aug 29 (Continued)	was rather heavily crossing the ridge E. of CRISSOLLES. The arty. suffered no casualties & retired via NOYON RIBÉCOURT to BAILLY - billeted.	
Sunday Aug 30th	The Div.l Artillery & Cav Div.n concentrated about COMPIEGNE. On the 3rd Bde with E Battery and D Battery - less 1 Sect. Batteries from this day are attached to Brigades of Cavalry 1 Battery to each Bde. Div Hq. left BAILLY at 9.15 a.m. & arrived at COMPIEGNE 2 pm.	
Monday Aug 31st	The Cav. Div.n covered the movement of the army to the West. Started at 4.30 a.m. Guns were not engaged the whole day. Got in touch with French Cav on our left flank & billeted at St VAAST.	
Tuesday Sept 1st	1st Cav Bde & L Battery RHA attacked in billets See Appendix B. The Div.n moved S. covering the retirement of the Infantry Div.ns to MONT L'EVEQUE - arrived 6.30 pm billeted. No engagement after the engagement in Appendix B.	See Appendix B.

WAR DIARY or INTELLIGENCE SUMMARY.

Army Form C. 2118.

Instructions regarding War Diaries and Intelligence Summaries are contained in F. S. Regs., Part II. and the Staff Manual respectively. Title pages will be prepared in manuscript.

(Erase heading not required.)

APPENDIX B

Hour, Date, Place	Summary of Events and Information	Remarks and references to Appendices
Tuesday September 7th	At 5.a.m the 1st Cav Bde & L Battery RHA were severely attacked in billets and bivouac at NERY by guns + maxim and rifle fire. The horses of L Battery RHA and The Bays were in bivouac and were either shot down or stampeded and lost. The men of the battery assisted their officers to get 3 guns into action 2 of which were immediately rendered useless by shell fire. The last gun served by 3 officers and Sergt Major and 1 Sergt with a gunner & driver carrying ammunition continued firing until the ammunition was expended and all the detachment except the Sergt Major were killed or wounded. The Regiments assisted this defence and the 4th Cav Bde and some of the regiments of the 4th Division supported the Bde and about 10.30 a.m the 5th D.Gds and Middlesex delivered a counter attack supported by the fire of the maxims & men of the 11th Hussars & Queens Bays & drove off the enemy with great loss & captured 8 guns. The guns were entrenched within 500 yards of the bivouacs. L Battery suffered very heavily. The guns were saved but 5 officers were killed, wounded & only S.M. Dorrell and 42 men are known to be saved. Major Sclater Booth Lts Giffard & Mundy wounded. Captain Bradbury & Lt Campbell killed. Gen Briggs recommends S.M. Dorrell and the gunner & driver for the Victoria Cross.	

WAR DIARY or INTELLIGENCE SUMMARY.

(Erase heading not required.)

Army Form C. 2118.

(6)

Hour, Date, Place	Summary of Events and Information	Remarks and references to Appendices
Wednesday September 2nd	The Divn. left its billets about MONTL'EVEQUE about 3.45 a.m. to make good communication with G.H.Q. towards DAMMARTIN. Raiding parties of enemy's Cavalry being reported in vicinity of ERMENONVILLE - 1st Cav Bde met a force of about 1000 Cav which retired N.W. precipitately & the Division captured 4 German guns. Billets at VILLENEUVE.	
Thursday Sept 3rd	Divn. started S at 4.30 am & marched to GOURNAY. No enemy encountered. Bivouaced S. of GOURNAY till 6pm. When the Cav. Divn. moved into billets in the neighbourhood of CHAMPS. H.Q. at Chateau CHAMPS.	
Friday Sept 4th	Halted all day to rest and refit. B.S.M. Dorrell. "L" Battery R.H.A. and details of this Battery amounting to 137 N.C.O's & men rejoined in the evening for transmission to base. Two four gun batteries were organised for the Cav. Divn. as follows. "I" Battery 4 guns. Major Thompson R.H.A. attached to 2nd Cav Bde. One sectn of "I" and one of "D" Battery, known hereafter as "Z" Battery to 1st Cav Bde. The 7th Bde R.H.A. Ammunition Coln formed two advanced mobile columns of limbered wagons only. All G.S. wagons remained with the Ammunition Column.	

WAR DIARY or INTELLIGENCE SUMMARY.

Army Form C. 2118.

(Erase heading not required.)

Hour, Date, Place	Summary of Events and Information	Remarks and references to Appendices
4.30 a.m 5th September 1914 to 9.15 pm	Left CHAMPS marched S.E to GRAMMAILLE — halted for 2 hours at midday & continued march to MORMANT — billeted. No enemy seen all day. 32nd Bde R.F.A. attached to Cav. Divn vice "L" Battery R.H.A.	
4.30 am 6th September 9 a.m. 8.30 pm	Left MORMANT as head of main body reached GASTINS the advanced guard met the adv. guard of a big German force at PECY. 2nd Cav Bde with I Battery RHA engaged — and enemy retired. 2nd Cav Bde was supported by 4th Cav Bde and Z battery. Billeted at JOUY le CHATEL	
7th September 7.30 pm	Started at 4.30 a.m & marched via LES ESSARTS — DAGNY — CHEVRU to CHOISY — but little opposition all day. Billeted at La HAUTE	
8th September 12 noon 2 pm 4.30 pm 6.30pm	Started 4.a.m. crossed R MARIN at JOUY & LA FERTE GAUCHERS with opposition. Crossed R. Le PETIT MARIN at SABLONNIERS — LE TRETOIRE & BELLOT. after a sharp fight enemy retiring in numbers of small columns up the long slopes towards N.E. 134 Battery & the Horse Artillery guns supported the crossing — after the crossing was effected I battery RHA got into action at massed Cavalry at 4000 yards about HONDEVILLIERS. 135 Battery supported a flanking movement by the 4th Cav Bde about BOIS du TARTRE with effect. To the farm at LE VOUE le PRETRE	

WAR DIARY
or
INTELLIGENCE SUMMARY.

Army Form C. 2118.

(8)

Hour, Date, Place	Summary of Events and Information	Remarks and references to Appendices
9th September 1.30 p.m. 7.30 p.m.	Started 4 a.m. Crossed River MARNE at AZY and NOGENT and advanced to MT. de BONNEIL & LE THIOLET. Found some 30 Germans in village of LUCY le BOCAGE all were taken or killed. Guns in action against retiring infantry and cavalry towards TORCY & BELLEAU. Went back to MT. de BONNEIL to billet.	
10th September 11 a.m. 1.30 p.m. 5 p.m.	Started 4 a.m. Whole division supported right flank of the 1st Divn in action westwards from MONTHIERS & passed on via BONNES - LATILLY to LA CROIX where large bodies of enemy's guns, cavalry, &c. moving were seen retreating N.E. All guns of division came into action about LA CROIX. Enemy had a battery in action behind OUCHY which was not located. Billeted at GRISOLLES	
11th September 5 a.m.	Crossed French Cav: Provisional Divn at OUCHY. Halted at SEVENAY at midday & then advanced to X rds N.E. ARCY. Guns not in action all day. Billets at SEVENAY.	
12th September 4.30 a.m. 2 p.m.	b X 25s. W/- Left SEVENAY & marched to RESCES - met opposition on the LE VESLE River. 1st Cav Bde supported by guns of R.H.A. pushed across the river. Divn followed. 1st Divn crossed & occupied high ground to N. Billeted at VAUXCERE	

WAR DIARY
or
INTELLIGENCE SUMMARY.
(Erase heading not required.)

Appendix C   Army Form C. 2118.

The Battle of the AISNE

Instructions regarding War Diaries and Intelligence Summaries are contained in F. S. Regs., Part II. and the Staff Manual respectively. Title pages will be prepared in manuscript.

Hour, Date, Place		Summary of Events and Information	Remarks and references to Appendices
September 13th	6 a.m.	The 2nd Cavalry Bde found the bridges over the canal and River AISNE at BOURG blown up. Supported by I Battery and guns of 32nd Bde RFA they forced the passage of the river with comparatively small losses and further drove the enemy out of the woods on to the high ground N of BOURG. G.O.C. 1st Army immediately supported and crossed the river with the whole of the fighting troops of the 1st Division secured the plateau 175 S.E. VERNEUIL supported by guns of 2nd Div & the 1st & 4th Cav Bdes above & E of PARGNAN. Hq of Cav. Div billeted at VILLERS.	
September 14th	4 a.m.	Was very foggy and in the fog the 1st Division & 1st Cavalry Division advanced and established themselves with heavy loss on the CHEMIN DES DAMES line from the X roads S of AILLES to the FABRIQUE near TROYON about which there was very heavy fighting. The 2nd Division on the left of the 1st Army about SOUPIR was held up & in reply to G.O.C. 1st Army the 1st & 2nd Cav Bdes with 2 Batteries RHA [Z & I] were sent to assist this flank. The guns of 32nd Bde RFA came into action about noon to support the attack on the CHEMIN DES DAMES with 135th Battery assisting French artillery in an artillery shelling of the big hill of Mt ROUGE which was held by German guns and infantry. Between 3 & 4 pm this artillery attack on the trenches of Moulin ROUGE was successful the enemy being observed vacating their trenches and retiring under very heavy fire & suffering great losses. The Zouaves then took the hill capturing about 100 prisoners. The 27th & 134 Batteries came into action about the TOURS DE PAISSY and materially assisted in repelling many counter attacks delivered against the position of the 1st Division who were entrenching some hundreds of yards S of the ridge of the CHEMIN DES DAMES. At nightfall the position was as above. Hq billets at VILLERS. At midday the Zouaves on the right of the 1st Div suddenly came back & 2 regiments of the 4th Cav Bde immediately took their place in the firing line.	
	12 noon		
	3 p.m.		

WAR DIARY
or
INTELLIGENCE SUMMARY.
(Erase heading not required.)

Army Form C. 2118.

Appendix C (cont'd)

Hour, Date, Place	Summary of Events and Information	Remarks and references to Appendices
September 15th 4.30 am 2. p.m.	Enemy steadily shelled the forward position of the 1st Div. all the early morning increasing later & systematically shelling the whole plateau of the TOURS DE PAISSY FERME. At 2 pm after a heavy bombardment the Germans delivered a serious counter attack all along the line but more strongly about the FABRIQUE at TROYON. The guns of the 32nd Bde from a position just S. of TOURS DE PAISSY F'me assisted to repel this attack by very fine shooting with most accurate range & fuze the enemy suffering heavy losses visibly from this accurate shell fire. Hq. billets VILLERS.	
September 16th 4.30 am 5 pm	Guns of 32nd Bde came into action 2 batteries S & 1 battery N of the TOURS DE PAISSY F.E. That battery N of F.E. assisting to support the French advance in the direction of HEUTEBISE F.E. and La CREUTE which was very slow & meeting with considerable opposition. The 2 batteries S of F.E. engaged enemy's battery or batteries in the neighbourhood of CERNY no accurate information was received from aeroplane or other sources. At 5 pm the guns of the 1st Division 2nd Division Cav Division & French 38th Div. shelled the enemy's position with searching fire for 20 minutes. Hq. billets VILLERS. The Cavalry Div. organised into 2 Divisions. 1st Div. consisting of 1st, 2nd & 4th Cavalry Bdes. with I, J, & L Batteries R.H.A. 2nd Div. consisting of 3rd & 5th Bdes with D & E Batteries R.H.A. J Battery joins from 5th Cav Bde, & sends one section to 'L' to replace the section of 'D' Battery, which rejoins its own unit. 'J' Battery is attached to 4th Cav Bde.	

WAR DIARY or INTELLIGENCE SUMMARY.

(Erase heading not required.)

Army Form C. 2118.

Appendix C (Cont'd)

Instructions regarding War Diaries and Intelligence Summaries are contained in F. S. Regs., Part II. and the Staff Manual respectively. Title pages will be prepared in manuscript.

Hour, Date, Place	Summary of Events and Information	Remarks and references to Appendices
September 17th 5 a.m.	The enemy heavily shelled the right of the 1st Division and the left of the French position as soon as it was light. Without any warning the Bde of Zouaves on the left of the French came back leaving a big gap. The 3rd Hussars & Composite regt of Household Cavalry were immediately ordered forward and the reserve batallion of the Queens Regt. reinforced & went straight into the trenches. The guns of the 32nd Bde supported from the same positions as on the 16th. They remained in action all day and were shooting steadily all the time - 2 batteries towards La CREUTE and the + road S. of AILLES & one battery at the FABRIQUE de TROYON.	
September 18th 9 a.m. 1 p.m.	1st & 12th Cav Bdes return to the 1st Cav Division the 7th Cav Bde to find 500 rifles daily the rest of the brigade resting in billets. The 32nd Brigade sent 2 batteries into action S of the TOURS DE PAISSY Fe. About 9.30 the Fe was very heavily shelled from the direction of AILLES by the heavy guns of enemy. Considerable casualties to the horses & Zouaves. They failed to reach the batteries which kept up a heavy fire with CERNY and AILLES as objective. About 1pm big guns in direction of CHAMOUILLE also located the batteries of 32nd Bde & shelled very heavily. The detachments were withdrawn - Two guns were hit directly and the batteries lost 2 killed & 20 wounded and about 10 horses killed This was found to be the work of spies. Guns were withdrawn without further loss after dark. Hqs billets VILLERS	

WAR DIARY or INTELLIGENCE SUMMARY.

Army Form C. 2118.

Appendix C (cont.)

Hour, Date, Place	Summary of Events and Information	Remarks and references to Appendices
September 19th	During night 18th–19th the right of the 7th Division was subjected to a strong night attack which was entirely unsuccessful & was repulsed chiefly by the Queens with heavy loss. The Cavalry Division artillery did not come into action. The French artillery was reinforced during night of 18th/19th & the 32nd Bde was not required & was held in reserve all day. Another Bde of Zouaves reinforced the French 38th Division and the 1st Division was reinforced this night by the 18th Infantry Brigade of the 6th Division. One Cavalry Bde only is used from this day on & the 7th Cav Bde still find 500 rifles. Gen Hq: required some shell to decide what guns were in action against us & the base of one of their biggest shells was found & sent to Gen Hq. The base measures 8½ inches across.	
September 20th Sunday	6am The Zouaves were subjected to active counter attacks from the enemy and somewhat easily were driven back. They were reinforced by 4 battalions and in addition the French Div: Gen: required the help of 2 squadrons of English cavalry. The right of the West Yorks finding the Zouaves retreating also fell back and Gen: de Lisle sent up 2 regiments of the 2nd Cav Bde to reestablish the situation which they did with great gallantry especially the 18th Dragoon Guards. The village of PAISSY was very heavily shelled in the morning from direction of AILLES. The 134 battery was brought into action just N of PARGNAN & the 135 just W of the TOURS de PAISSY road to endeavour to slacken this shelling which they did. The 29th Batty was held in readiness to occupy a position S of TOURS de PAISSY Fm to engage enemy about Mt VAUXCERE. Hq which VILLERS.	

WAR DIARY or **INTELLIGENCE SUMMARY.**

Army Form C. 2118.

Appendix C (cont'd)

Instructions regarding War Diaries and Intelligence Summaries are contained in F. S. Regs., Part II. and the Staff Manual respectively. Title pages will be prepared in manuscript.

(Erase heading not required.)

Hour, Date, Place	Summary of Events and Information	Remarks and references to Appendices
September 21st 5 am 5 p.m.	The 134 Battery and 27th Battery were brought into action N of PARGNAM to engage the batteries reported about CERNY with 135 Battery in reserve. The French were attacking HURTEBISE about 10 am when they came under a very heavy shell fire from the ridge due N of La CREUTE. J Battery were in action on the plateau N of PAISSY and in order to reduce this shelling a section 135th Battery were sent to PAISSY to assist J Battery & to try & enfilade the batteries N of La CREUTE. This section came into action under heavy shell fire and remained in action for over an hour being very heavily shelled all the time but eventually were forced to withdraw detachments & leave guns to be withdrawn under cover of darkness. 4 men killed 5 wounded & several horses killed. J Battery were unable to fight their guns after 2 pm owing to the heavy shell fire. The How.d. Bde of the 7th Divn. also at PAISSY suffered somewhat heavily in horses & slightly in personnel as well. 2 guns of J Battery & 1 gun & 2 wagons of 135 Batty were hit. Otherwise the shelling was not severe during the day. Hq billet at VILLERS	
September 22nd 1 pm	Desultory shelling all morning. At 1 pm the heavy guns of enemy endeavoured to knock out French & English artillery N of PARGNAM. For 2 hours the slope was subjected to continuous and heavy shell fire. Cav Div. Hq. were shelled severely & moved further to &. The detachments of the French & English batteries were withdrawn under cover and the casualties were small. Some damage was done to the houses at the E end of the village of PARGNAM. F.M. C. in C. came to visit the 1st Cav Div. & was shown the situation in the plateau of the TOURS de PAISSY F.. Hq. billet VILLERS	

WAR DIARY
or
INTELLIGENCE SUMMARY.

(Erase heading not required.)

Army Form C. 2118.

Appendix C (continued)

Hour, Date, Place	Summary of Events and Information	Remarks and references to Appendices
September 23rd 10 a.m. 4-5 pm	The guns of 32nd Use occupied the same positions N of PARGNAM at 5 am. At 10 a.m the aeroplanes of the French & English Flying Corps reported that a triangle just N of the CHEMIN DES DAMES extending from apex at TROYON FABRIQUE with its base S of S in LAONNOIS was full of enemy's guns. All guns of the Car Div. shelled this triangle and forced enemy's batteries to move. Toward evening the enemy again heavily shelled positions of the guns N of PARGNAN and also located Div Hd Staff and shelled them also. Nearly all this bombardment was carried out by the heavy guns firing high Explosive. Hqrs billet VILLERS.	
September 24th 11. a.m. 6 pm	Owing to shelling of last 2 days the J.H. Arty Batteries changed their positions the 27th Batty occupied a positn in orchard just W of N in PARGNAN and 135 Batty a position due N of CIASSY Fme Excellent aeroplane reports both French & English disclosed the position of the enemy's batteries which were heavily shelled and further reports disclosed their secondary positions taken up after being shelled out of 1st posn. Usual shelling of the PARGNAN ridge at 5pm by high Explosives but no battery was discovered or hit & the bombardment ceased at dusk having accomplished nothing. The 1st Car Bde cease to find two rifles and 1 regiment only instead of 1 brigade is on duty daily from this date on. Remainder Car Div rest rept in billets. Hqrs billet VILLERS.	

WAR DIARY
or
INTELLIGENCE SUMMARY.
(Erase heading not required.)

Army Form C. 2118.

Instructions regarding War Diaries and Intelligence Summaries are contained in F. S. Regs., Part II. and the Staff Manual respectively. Title pages will be prepared in manuscript.

Hour, Date, Place	Summary of Events and Information	Remarks and references to Appendices
Sept 25th	134th and 135th Batteries R.F.A. proceeded at 5.30 am to rendezvous at CIASSY Fm, E of DEUILLY. 27th Battery remained in billets. 134th Battery in action N of PARGNAN. 135th in action W of CIASSY Fm. H.Q. billet at VILLERS.	
Sept 26th	27th & 134th Batteries proceeded at 5.30 am N of PARGNAN. The 134th came into action just N of village. 27th Battery in reserve. 135th Battery in billets. H.Q. billet at VILLERS	
Sept 27th	Brigade remained in billets, 134th Battery saddled up ready to turn out. 1st Cav. Bde moved out in support of Guards' Brigade at SOUPIR, accompanied by "I" Battery R.H.A. Returned to billets in the early hours of the 28th. H.Q. billet at VILLERS	
Sept 28th	"J" and "I" Batteries again made up to 6 guns and "L" Battery abolished. "H" Battery joined 1st Cav Divn and attached to 2nd Cav Bde. H.Q. billet at VILLERS.	
Sept 29th	2nd Cav. Bde shelled in their billets at LONGUEVAL. 9th Lancers had 1 officer + 26 men killed & wounded. "H" Battery 1 man wounded. H.Q. billet at VILLERS	
Sept 30th	2nd Cav. Bde & "H" Battery move from LONGUEVAL and billet at BAZOCHES. H.Q. billet at VILLERS.	

HD. QRS.
1st CAV. DIV.
2.10.14

William Jelf
Capt R.H.A.
Staff Capt
1st Cav Div Arty

1st Cavalry Divisional Artillery.

C. R. A.

1st CAVALRY DIVISION.

1st to 12th OCTOBER 1914.

WAR DIARY
or
INTELLIGENCE SUMMARY.
(Erase heading not required.)

Army Form C. 2118.

Hour, Date, Place	Summary of Events and Information	Remarks and references to Appendices
Oct 1st	The 1st Cav Div remained in billets. 2nd Cav Bde is placed temporarily under the direct orders of the 1st Corps. H.Q. Billet VILLERS	
Oct 2nd	1st Cav Div remained in billets, with 4th Cav Bde ready to turn out if ordered. 32nd Bde R.F.A ordered to rejoin the 4th Div	
Oct 3rd	Moved to the neighbourhood of BRAINE at 8am. H.Q. billet at that place. 8 miles	
Oct 4th	8pm 1st Cav Div continued its march westwards. 12 midnight the H.Q. arrived at VILLERS-HELON and billeted at Chateau. 15 miles. Ammunition Col at PLESSIERS-HULEU. "I" Battery R.H.A at VILLERS-HELON. "H" Battery at TIGNY. "J" Battery at ST REMY.	
Oct 5th	8pm 1st Cav Div continued its march via VILLERS-COTTERET to RUSSY. Arrived about 1am on 6th. H.Q. billet in RUSSY. H Battery billet at HARAMONT. I Battery billet at MORIENVAL. J Battery at CREPY EN VALOIS. 18 miles. Fine night.	
Oct 6th	March continued at 12 noon to JANQUIERE. Arrived at 6pm. H.Q. billet at JANQUIERE. Dull weather.	
Oct 7th	March continued to MONTDIDIER. Fine day. On arrival at that place at 12 noon, the Cav Div took up a position of readiness to assist the 10 French Corps if necessary.	

WAR DIARY or INTELLIGENCE SUMMARY.

Army Form C. 2118.

Hour, Date, Place	Summary of Events and Information	Remarks and references to Appendices
Oct 7th (continued)	1st Cav. Bde to a point W of the road FAVEROLLES – ETHELFAY & just N of railway. 2nd Cav. Bde to W side of ETHELFAY. 4th Cav. Bde to N of 1st Div in MONTDIDIER. Our assistance was not required and at 3.30pm the Div was ordered to billets. HQ billet at FONTAINE. 30 miles. Arrived 5pm.	
Oct 8th	The march was continued northwards at 9am via AMIENS to ARGOEUVE. Fine day. 29 miles. H Battery billet at VILLERS BOCAGE. I Battery in VAUX en AMIENOIS. J Battery in BERTANGLES. Arrived 4.30pm. HQ billet at ARGOEUVE	
Oct 9th	March continued northwards via DOULLENS to REBREUVE. Fine day. Arrived 4.30pm. 30 miles. HQ billet at REBREUVE.	
Oct 10th	March continued north to CHELERS. Short march of 12 miles. Left at 9.30am. Arrived at 12.30pm. HQ billet at Chateau. Dull day, with cold wind.	
Oct 11th	March continued towards LILLERS, at 7.30am. Short march of 14 miles. Arrived 10.45am. Movement continued at 3pm to St VENANT where H.Q. billeted for night.	

WAR DIARY
or
INTELLIGENCE SUMMARY.

(Erase heading not required.)

Army Form C. 2118.

Hour, Date, Place	Summary of Events and Information	Remarks and references to Appendices
October 12th	German patrols are reported in the direction of NEUF BERQUIN and VIEUX BERQUIN, and on the high ground about LE MT. des CATS. The 2nd Cav. Div. is on the line HAZEBROUCK, WALLON-CAPPEL. The 1st Cav. Div. concentrated at VIERHOUCK and VERTE RUE, with H.Q. at ROUSSEL FARM. The Germans were engaged all along the road NEUF BERQUIN — VIEUX BERQUIN and Lieut Edwards, I Battery was killed. Billeted at Château La MOTTE. Orders received for formation of Cavalry corps, under command of Maj. Gen. Allenby.